D0512565

The
Mountain
Book

SECOND EDITION

Glacier lake

⚠ Take care in mountains!

Mountains are some of the world's most exciting landscapes and you are sure to want to visit them. But never go up mountains without the correct clothing and footwear and without a qualified and experienced mountain leader. Remember, mountain environments can be dangerous and deaths have occurred because people have gone walking unprepared. You must never take risks near snow or on steep slopes.

Cattle on high Alpine pastures in summer

Curriculum Visions

There's much more on-line including videos

You will find multimedia resources covering a wide range of topics in the Professional Zone at:

www.CurriculumVisions.com

A CVP Book
This second edition © Earthscape 2008

First edition 2000

Author
Brian Knapp, BSc, PhD

Art Director
Duncan McCrae, BSc

Senior Designer
Adele Humphries, BA, PGCE

Editors
Mary Sanders, BSc, and Gillian Gatehouse

Designed and produced by
EARTHSCAPE

Printed in China by
WKT Company Ltd

The Mountain Book Second Edition – Curriculum Visions
A CIP record for this book is available from the British Library

Paperback ISBN 978 1 86214 551 1

Illustrations
All illustrations by *David Woodroffe* except the following: *Nicolas Debon* 5; *Julian Baker* 7t.

Picture credits
All photographs are from the Earthscape Picture Library except the following (c=centre t=top b=bottom l=left r=right): *Corbis* 3, 23bl, 43tr, 45br; *NASA* 9tl, 19b; *ShutterStock* 1, 2, 3; *USGS* 45cr.

This product is manufactured from sustainable managed forests. For every tree cut down at least one more is planted.

Contents

Ibex are extremely agile and well suited to steep mountain slopes

The mountain environment

Mountains are rugged and harsh and so seem to be unaffected by people. Yet they are actually very fragile environments. Here is an overview of the main features described in this book.

A mountain is high ground that rises more than 300 metres above the surrounding landscape **❶**. Most mountains occur in groups called mountain ranges **❷**), which form larger groups called mountain chains.

Some mountains are formed by volcanoes. But most are formed by when plates of the earth's crust collide.

Mountains are worn away by rivers and glaciers **❸**. When glaciers melt, they leave U-shaped valleys with sheer sides. Waterfalls and long finger lakes then form **❹**.

It is much colder and windier, and the weather is far more changeable on mountains than on plains **❺**. Heavy rain and snow fall on slopes facing the wind, but the sheltered slopes may be deserts.

Avalanches, blizzards and snowdrifts are the main winter hazards **❻**.

The plants found on mountain tops are different from those in the valleys **❼**. Animals have to adapt to survive with little food in harsh mountain areas **❽**.

People have to adapt to the harsh winters, too. Farming can be difficult in mountains, especially in winter **❾❿**. Travelling through mountain areas can be a problem because of the many steep slopes and narrow valleys **❿**.

People have built special kinds of homes so that they can live comfortably in the mountains **⓫**. But people can also be a threat to mountain environments when they use them for winter sports **⓭**, for summer holidays and for camping.

▶ ① **This diagram shows all of the major natural and man-made features of a mountain environment.**

◀ ② **This is a view in the Alps during summer. Compare it with picture** ① **and see how many features labelled in picture** ① **you can identify in this photograph..**

What are mountains?

Mountains have peaks and steep slopes that stand high above the surrounding countryside.

What does the word mountain mean to you? Do you immediately think of Mount Everest, the world's highest peak, rising to 8,848 metres? Do you think of tall cone-shaped volcanoes with snowcapped summits and plumes of smoke? Or do you think of tall ranges of peaks that stretch for thousands of kilometres?

In fact, all of these are mountains. Mountains are parts of the landscape with steep slopes that rise 300 metres or more above their surroundings.

Where mountains are found

Mountains are found all over the world. Volcanoes usually stand alone. They make most of the islands in the world's oceans. Most mountains, however, make long high ridges called mountain ranges (pictures ① and ②).

▼ ① **This diagram shows some of the highest mountain peaks and highest volcanoes on each continent and in the oceans. All heights are in metres above sea level. Their locations are shown on the map at the top of page 7.**

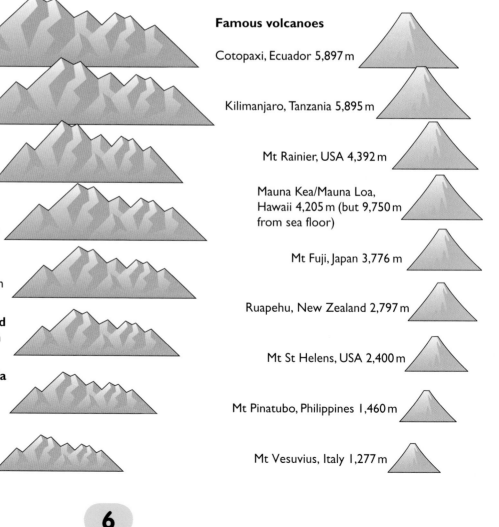

Mountain chains

Himalayas, Asia
Mt Everest, Nepal/Tibet 8,848 m

Andes, South America
Aconcagua, Argentina/Chile 6,959 m

Rockies, North America
Mt McKinley, USA 6,194 m

Antartica
Vinson Massif 4,897 m

Alps, Europe
Mont Blanc, France/Italy 4,807 m

Southern Alps, New Zealand
Mt Cook, New Zealand 3,765 m

Great Dividing Range, Australia
Mt Kosciusko, Australia 2,230 m

United Kingdom
Ben Nevis, Scotland 1,344 m
Snowdon, Wales 1,085 m
Scafell Pike, England 978 m
Slieve Donard, Northern Ireland 850 m

Famous volcanoes

Cotopaxi, Ecuador 5,897 m

Kilimanjaro, Tanzania 5,895 m

Mt Rainier, USA 4,392 m

Mauna Kea/Mauna Loa, Hawaii 4,205 m (but 9,750 m from sea floor)

Mt Fuji, Japan 3,776 m

Ruapehu, New Zealand 2,797 m

Mt St Helens, USA 2,400 m

Mt Pinatubo, Philippines 1,460 m

Mt Vesuvius, Italy 1,277 m

Rockies

Alps

Himalayas

Andes

Great Dividing Range

Southern Alps

Famous volcanoes
1 Cotopaxi, Ecuador
2 Kilimanjaro, Tanzania
3 Mt Rainier, USA
4 Mauna Kea/Mauna Loa, Hawaii
5 Mt Fuji, Japan
6 Ruapehu, New Zealand
7 Mt St Helens, USA
8 Mt Pinatubo, Philippines
9 Mt Vesuvius, Italy

▲ ② The world's largest land mountains are arranged in long chains. There is also a range of mountains within the world's oceans, but this lies mainly below sea level and so is out of sight.

Iceland

North America

Europe

Atlantic Ocean

Mid-Atlantic Ridge

Africa

South America

Antarctica

◄ ③ The world's longest mountain chain is 16,000 km long and lies below the Atlantic Ocean. Although the peaks are high, the ocean is so deep that the peaks only reach the surface in a few places, such as Iceland. The peaks on this chain are all volcanoes.

The Lake District in northwestern England, Snowdonia in northern Wales, the Mourne Mountains in Northern Ireland and the Cairngorms in northeastern Scotland, are all mountain ranges.

When many ranges stretch for thousands of kilometres, they make up a mountain chain. The Alps in Europe, the Himalayas in Asia, the Andes in South America, and the Rocky Mountains in North America are all mountain chains (picture ③).

Mountain chains

Mountain chains form when parts of the earth's crust collide.

Most of the world's mountains are not volcanoes, but long chains of folded rocks. How did they form? To understand this, you have to know that the surface of the Earth is just a thin crust of solid rock (picture ①) floating on molten rock below.

▲ ① **The Earth's crust is cracked into a number of plates floating on molten rock.**

▶ ② **The plates are moved over the earth by churning forces inside the Earth. Where plates collide, rocks are folded into ranges and volcanoes erupt.**

Colliding plates crumple at the edges to make mountain chains. This is the Andes.

Molten rock within the earth pushes plates together.

Folding in rocks caused by plates colliding

Matterhorn

Switzerland

Italy

Plate

Plate

◀ ③ **The crumpled plate edges are very folded. This shows a cross-section through the Alps.**

▼ ④ Fold mountains are formed on a grand scale. This can be imagined by pushing on a tablecloth from two directions (see below). In this example, ranges have been produced in the shape of the Rocky Mountains of North America. The picture on the left shows the real mountains, as viewed from a Space Shuttle.

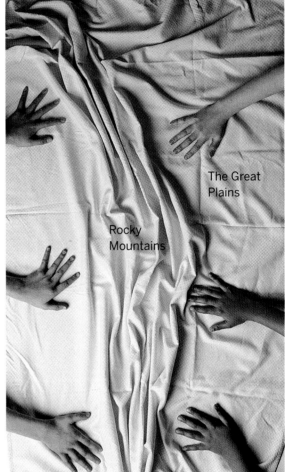

The Great Plains

Rocky Mountains

This crust is broken into huge slabs, rather like the surface of a cracked eggshell. These slabs, called plates, are being pulled about by the churning movements of the molten rock below (picture ②) rather like the skin on a gently simmering soup. As the plates are dragged along, some of them collide. This causes the edges of the plates to crumple up just like when two cars crash – only it takes hundreds of millions of years to happen. This is what makes the rocks at the edge fold into long mountain chains (pictures ③ and ④).

At the plate edges

We know where the plate edges are because this is where the rocks are folding. The rock is brittle and so it tends to crack as well as fold. Each crack makes an earthquake. Sometimes the cracks also let molten rock reach the surface, causing a volcano. So places with earthquakes and volcanoes mark the edges of the world's giant plates. At the moment, most of the active land volcanoes are around the Pacific Ocean. The pattern they make there has been called the Pacific Ring of Fire.

Volcanoes

Volcanoes are made when molten rock and ash explode out of the ground.

Volcanoes are places where magma (molten rock) flows out of, or explodes from, the ground. If this happens time and time again, a volcanic mountain will grow (picture ①).

▼ ① This diagram shows the main features of a volcano and how it is connected to the magma chamber below. Notice that there are many lines of weakness above the magma chamber. If more than one weakness is opened up, then several volcanoes can erupt side by side. Sometimes small vents open on the flanks of the volcano. When this happens, small cones build and the main volcano loses its balanced shape.

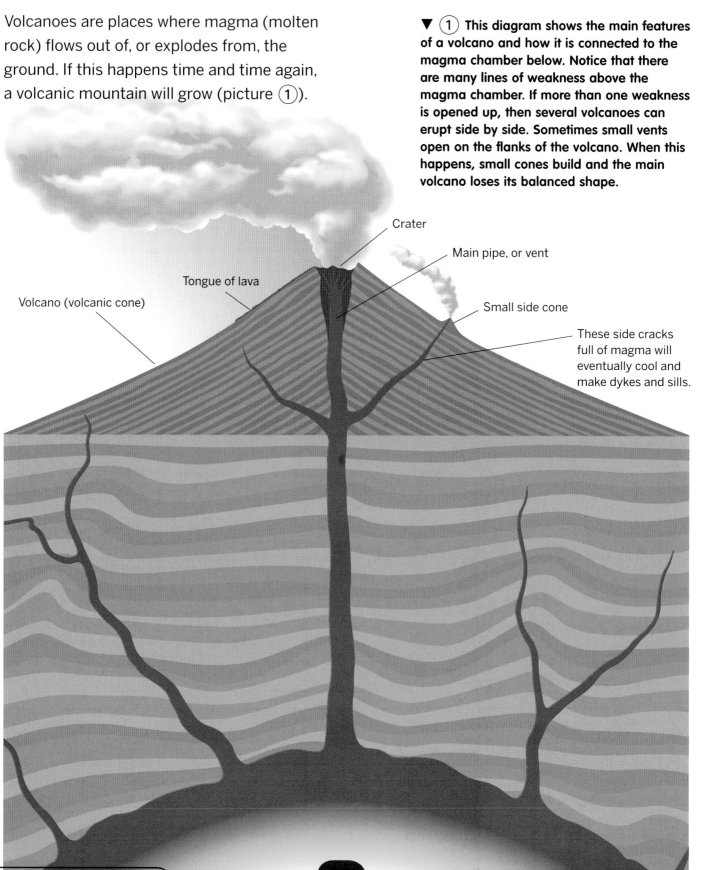

Crater

Main pipe, or vent

Tongue of lava

Small side cone

Volcano (volcanic cone)

These side cracks full of magma will eventually cool and make dykes and sills.

Inside a volcano

If you could look inside a volcano, you would find a vast chamber of molten rock deep underground. This is where the liquid rock (lava) (picture ②) and ash come from.

Vent and crater

Many volcanoes are conical mountains with a pit in the top, called a crater (picture ③).

A volcano of this kind is fed by a great, circular chimney, called a vent. As the erupting volcano throws out, or ejects, material, it builds up a cone around itself.

Mountains of layers

Volcanic mountains are built from the materials they spew out during eruptions.

Few mountains are made entirely of lava. Normally they are also made of layers of fine rock fragments. Most explosive eruptions send great volumes of rock fragments, such as fine ash, high into the sky. Some of it lands back on the volcano.

In this way, each eruption may create a layer of ash and a layer of lava to add to the mountain. Over thousands of years this can build mountains thousands of metres high.

▲ ③ The crater area at the top of a volcano.

▶ ② Lava eruption on Kilauea Volcano, Hawaiian islands

Gas and ash

Layers

Magma chamber

Dangerous explosions

Some volcanoes explode almost without warning, sending fiery gases and ash across the nearby land.

Many volcanoes go through a cycle of events, with an eruption followed by a quiet spell. An eruption happens when the pressure in the full magma chamber is so great that magma can force its way to the surface, and open the vent again.

At first, the eruption throws out huge amounts of scalding gases, boiling water, ash and fragments of rock (pictures ①, ② and ④). These make towering clouds over the volcano.

Eventually, however, there is no longer enough pressure to push magma up the vent, and so the magma stops rising to the surface.

At the surface, gas bubbles expand explosively and send magma out as a fine spray, which cools mostly to ash, with some cinders and volcanic bombs.

Near the surface, the weight of the magma is lower and that allows gas bubbles to grow.

Deep in the vent, the magma is under pressure and the gas remains mostly dissolved in the magma.

▲ ① **This shows the way in which ash is formed near the top of the vent.**

▼ ② **Probably the most stunning view that you can see on Earth is an explosive eruption in progress. This view was taken during the first minute of an eruption, looking at the side of the mountain that was blasted away.**

It may take anything from a few days to a few months for this to happen. Finally, the last of the magma starts to cool in the vent, and that plugs the volcano and it gets quiet again.

Dormant means danger

While a volcano is refilling its magma chamber, it is dormant (sleeping). As the magma chamber refills, the pressure of the magma will cause earthquakes and they will weaken the rock above. They also warn people of danger, for the magma may find a route to the surface through the weakened side of the mountain. When this happens, the blast will go sideways over the surrounding land. In 1980, Mt St Helens blew up like this after more than a century of being dormant (pictures ③ and ⑤).

▲ ④ The large piece is a volcanic bomb that weighs about 500 g. See how it is partly moulded from its travel through the air. The smaller pieces are cinders. Each weighs about 20 g. Notice that the marks on the surface show where gas bubbles in the molten rock have burst.

▼ ⑤ This car belonged to some people who did not manage to escape. The car was crushed by the force of the gases and ash in the exploding volcano.

▼ ③ This picture was taken from high above the volcano after the eruption had ended. The picture looks straight down on the volcano and sets out the scene just like a map. The green area on the left is untouched forest. The grey area on the right has no forest left, just bare soil. The right-hand side of the volcano has been blown away.

Ice in the mountains

Peaks, ridges and valleys – all show ice and frost at work.

Many mountain landscapes have sharp peaks, knife-edged ridges and deep, U-shaped valleys. These sharp edges are formed by frost, while the deep smoothed-out valleys and mountain hollows are scoured by the scraping action of glaciers (pictures ①, ②, ③).

Frost action

Frost changes the shape of high mountains. In spring and autumn it is often warm by day, but freezing cold by night. If rain falls in the day and seeps into cracks, it will freeze overnight. As the water freezes, it swells and prises rocks apart. This happens year after year, sending broken rocks down into the valleys to make a jumble of sharp-edged rocks called scree, and leaving steep, jagged peaks and knife-edged ridges.

A pointed peak, also called a horn, is produced by several glaciers eating into the sides of a mountain summit.

Bowl-shaped mountain hollow scoured by ice. It is called a corrie or cirque.

Debris is plucked off the valley floor by the ice and is then used like sandpaper to scour deeper into the valley floor.

▼ ① **A typical mountain landscape from the Canadian Rocky Mountains.**

Mountainside hollow (also called a corrie)

Pyramidal peak

Ridge (also called an arete)

▼ **This diagram shows the main features of a glaciated valley.**

Glaciers scour a U-shaped valley (see page 12).

A small tributary valley filled with ice. It is called a hanging valley (see page 14).

Mountain slopes above the ice are made steeper by frost shatter.

A sharp-sided ridge, or arete, formed as two valleys are widened by glaciers.

Glacier

This debris from the glacier is called moraine.

Glaciers

When snow builds up into great thicknesses, it turns into ice. The ice then flows downhill under its own weight. A tongue of ice is called a glacier. Glaciers in small valleys flow together to fill a main valley, just as small streams gather to make a river.

As a glacier flows, any broken rock sticks to its underside and scrapes away at the rock of the valley floor. This erosion changes the shape of the valley, making it steep-sided and flat-bottomed, that is U-shaped.

◄ ③ **The U-shaped Morteratsch glacier melting during the summer, Alps.**

15

Mountain valleys and waterfalls

The valleys left by glaciers are straight; they have almost sheer sides and many waterfalls.

The Ice Age

In the recent past, the world was much colder – a time known as the Ice Age. During this time, glaciers formed on the slopes of mountains and flowed into valleys that had once been cut by rivers.

U-shaped valleys

As glaciers wore away the landscape, they changed the shape of the valleys (picture ①) from narrow V-shapes to wide, flat-bottomed U-shapes. This is why ice-scoured valleys are called U-shaped valleys.

Hanging valleys

A big glacier scours its valley floor much faster than a small one. So, glaciers in the main valleys cut down more deeply than glaciers in the small valleys that flow into them.

You cannot see this when the valleys are still filled with ice. But, when the ice melts away, you can see the smaller valleys left 'hanging' high up the sheer sides of the main valley. This is why they are called hanging valleys.

Since the last Ice Age, the weather has become warmer and the glaciers have melted away from all but the highest mountains. Streams flow in the valley bottoms again. Those that flow along tributaries often fall from the edge of the hanging valley on to the floor of the main valley, making spectacular waterfalls (picture ②).

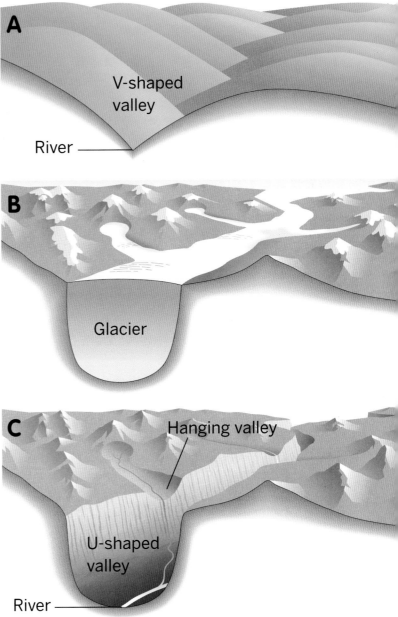

▲ ① **(A) Before the Ice Age, rivers cut V-shaped valleys.**

During the Ice Age, ice filled the valleys and scoured them into a new shape, much broader than before, and with a flat floor.

(B) Parts of the mountains left above the ice formed jagged pyramidal peaks and sharp ridges.

(C) When the Ice Age ended, rivers flowed in the valleys again. Waterfalls formed where tributaries fell to the main valley floors.

▼▶ ② This is the Yosemite Valley in the Sierra Nevada mountains of California, United States. The valley is U-shaped, with sheer sides and a flat floor. The valley slopes rise over 1,100 m from the river.

The valley is so straight that you can see right along it. There is a hanging valley on the right of the picture below, with a waterfall coming from it (called the Bridalveil Falls).

The diagram on the right shows what Yosemite Valley might have looked like when it was full of ice during the last Ice Age. The glacier in the main valley has been cut away to help you see how hanging valleys formed. The waterfalls and rivers you can see today are also shown, although they would only have formed after the ice had melted away completely.

Ice-filled tributary valley. When the ice melts a waterfall will form where it meets the main valley.

Glacier

Yosemite Valley

Site of river

Bridalveil Falls

17

Mountain lakes and passes

In mountain areas, finger lakes and passes often form where glaciers once flowed.

When ice moves through a valley, it scours at the rock below it. If the rock is hard, the ice wears away slowly, but if the rock is soft, the ice scours more quickly (picture ①).

Finger lakes

Ice moves like toothpaste in a tube. It is pushed through a valley by the weight of the ice in the mountains. This means that ice can flow into and out of a hollow. But water cannot do this. So, when the ice melts and rivers once again flow in mountain valleys, they fill up the hollows to make long, narrow lakes called ribbon lakes, or finger lakes (picture ②).

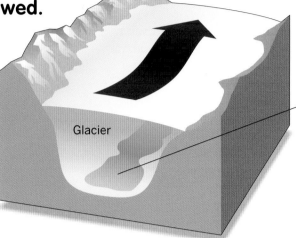

Glacier

Ice scours more deeply into softer rock. A lake will form here when ice melts.

▲ ① **A finger lake can form in a valley after the ice has melted away at the end of the Ice Age.**

▼ ② **Here are two finger lakes. They are Buttermere (foreground) and Crummock Water (background) in the English Lake District. They were once a single lake, but a river on the right has carried silt into the lake, where it has settled out and formed a delta. The delta has grown right across the lake. In time, as more material settles out in the lakes, they will be completely filled in.**

▶ ③ A pass is formed when ice spills between valleys.

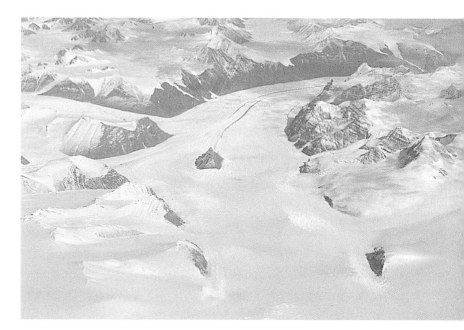

Passes

If a valley fills up with ice and then spills over its sides, the route it takes between the valleys will be scoured away too (picture ③). When the ice melts away, deep trenches are left that cut right across the mountain ranges (picture ④). These are used as passes because they give the easiest route across the mountains.

Ice flows from one valley into the next, scouring a U-shaped trench.

▼▶ ④ The famous pass of Glen Coe, Scotland was created when a glacier spilled across a mountain range and flowed on towards the sea. This view looks in the direction that the ice flowed. You can see the U-shape of this trench very clearly.

Mountain weather

Mountains are cold, harsh, windy places where the weather changes faster than anywhere else in the world.

Mountains are colder (picture ③), winds are stronger, snow is more common and the weather changes more quickly than on lowlands (picture ②).

High and cold

The highest mountains have a permanent **SNOWLINE**, because at these **ALTITUDES** the air is always below freezing (picture ①).

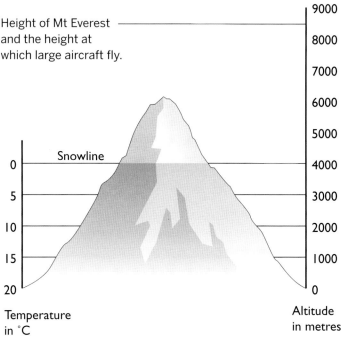

Height of Mt Everest and the height at which large aircraft fly.

Snowline

Temperature in °C

Altitude in metres

▲ ① The higher up a mountain you go, the colder it gets. On average it is 5°C colder for each 1,000 m of height. This means that it is always below freezing on the world's highest mountains, which explains why they are always snowcapped.

◄ ② Those who are used to the mountains often say that you can have all four seasons in one day.
   These two pictures show exactly how fast the weather can change. The bottom one was taken just two minutes after the one above. A blizzard set in on the sunny ski-slopes (called pistes) before anyone had time to seek shelter.

▲ ③ The higher up a mountain you go, the colder it gets. This means that winters last far longer on mountains than in nearby lowlands. The snowline gives you a guide as to where freezing point is.

Rainshadows

The sides of mountains facing the wind (the windward side) often have much more cloud, rain and snow than those on the sheltered (lee) sides of mountains (picture ④). This is called a rainshadow effect.

As winds blow over a mountain range, the air gets cooler. Cool air can hold less moisture than warm air, and what can't be held is turned into tiny water droplets.

This produces cloud. The droplets gather together inside the cloud to make raindrops or ice crystals (snow).

When the air has crossed the highest peaks, it begins to sink and the air warms. Now it can hold the moisture that remains. This is why far side of the mountains therefore receives much less rain. This is called a rainshadow.

◄▼ ④ The side of a mountain facing moist winds is often called the 'weather side' because it is cloudier, has more rain and is more changeable than the sheltered side.

The weather data are taken from the south (chart A) and north (chart B) sides of the Himalayas. They show a rainshadow effect at its most extreme. The place on the rain-drenched side in the south gets tens of times more rain than the place in the rainshadow to the north.

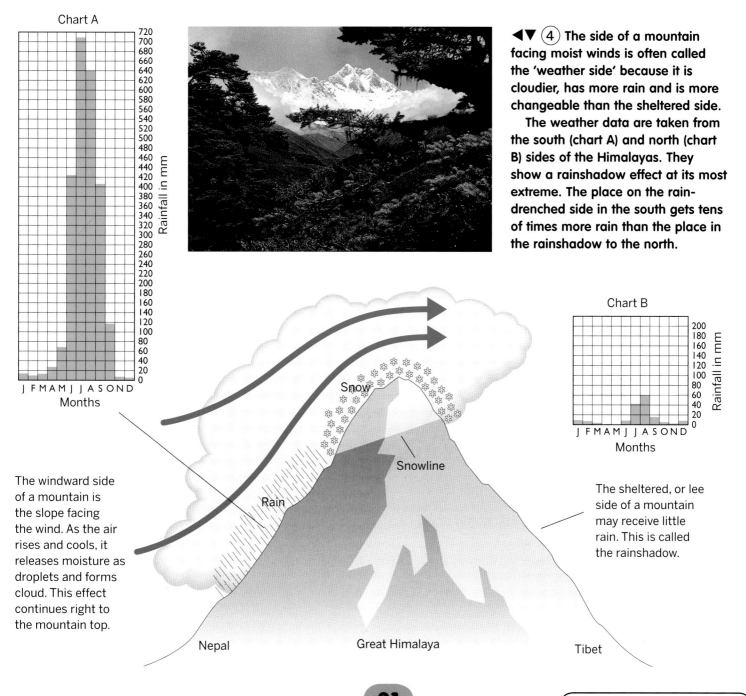

Chart A

Rainfall in mm

J F M A M J J A S O N D
Months

Chart B

Rainfall in mm

J F M A M J J A S O N D
Months

Snow

Snowline

Rain

The windward side of a mountain is the slope facing the wind. As the air rises and cools, it releases moisture as droplets and forms cloud. This effect continues right to the mountain top.

The sheltered, or lee side of a mountain may receive little rain. This is called the rainshadow.

Nepal

Great Himalaya

Tibet

Blizzards and avalanches

A combination of strong winds and heavy snowfall creates blizzards, while snowdrifts can suddenly break free and become avalanches.

The higher you go up a mountain, the more the snow that falls. Snow is over twelve times as bulky as rain and it settles on the surface, rather than sinking into the soil. This is why snow forms deep enough to bury houses (picture ①).

Snowdrifts

Snowflakes are like tiny sails. Even gentle winds can carry snow along. Snow rarely settles on steep, windward mountain faces, but rather on the sheltered sides, or in valleys.

Once snowflakes have landed, their star-like shapes lock together and also hold fast on the ground. In this way, snow builds upon snow to form huge banks, or snowdrifts, that pile up against and behind obstacles (picture ②).

▲ ① **Snowdrifts can almost bury villages in the mountains.**

▼ ② **Snow piles up behind, and to a smaller extent in front of, anything that stands up in a snowstorm.**

Blizzards

Mountain peaks often funnel wind between them and make the wind stronger.

In these strong winds, the snowflakes gets turned into tiny balls of ice and a snowfall becomes a blizzard.

A blizzard is a snowstorm with winds that blow faster than 50 kilometres an hour. You can often see less than 150 metres in a blizzard.

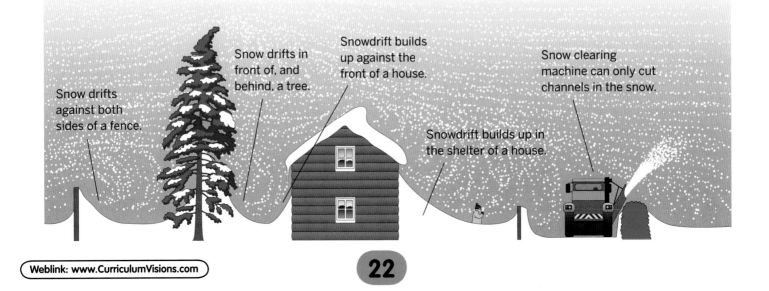

Snow drifts against both sides of a fence.

Snow drifts in front of, and behind, a tree.

Snowdrift builds up against the front of a house.

Snow clearing machine can only cut channels in the snow.

Snowdrift builds up in the shelter of a house.

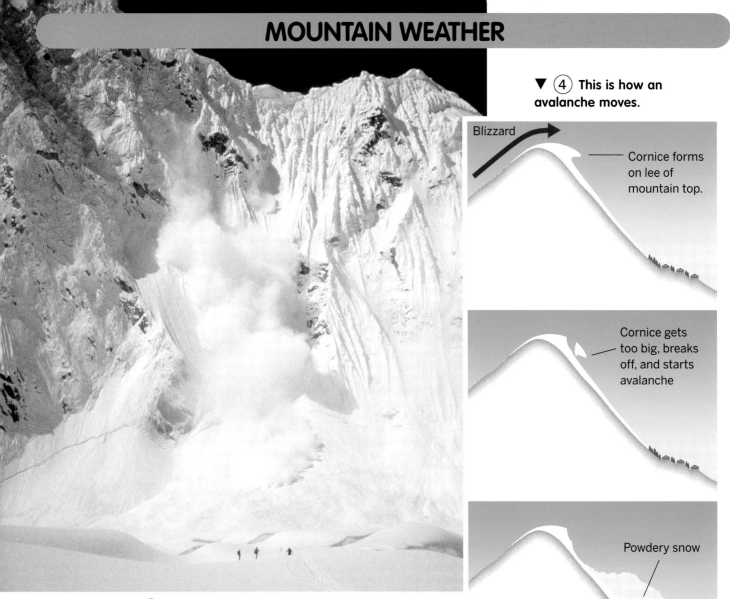

▼ ④ **This is how an avalanche moves.**

Blizzard

Cornice forms on lee of mountain top.

Cornice gets too big, breaks off, and starts avalanche

Powdery snow

Main avalanche

Avalanche destroys trees and houses, often burying them

▲ ③ **An avalanche in motion on Mt Everest.**

Avalanches

An avalanche is a huge mass of snow on the move (picture ③). Avalanches can contain millions of tonnes of snow and move at over 300 kilometres an hour.

Avalanches are most common on moderately steep slopes (picture ④). Here the snow is thick and eventually it will move under its own weight. Each storm adds a new layer of snow to the slope. You can think of snow on a mountainside as being like sheets of paper on a slope. As the snow gets thicker and heavier, the layers give way and then the rest of the snow begins to move – the avalanche has started.

As the snow slides forward it breaks up and flows like water. At the same time, loose snow is lifted off the surface and makes a cloud of snow above it (picture ③) that moves at the speed of an express train.

Ski resorts

Winter sports depend on just the right combination of mountain weather.

Many people take winter sports holidays. But only a few places are favourite destinations for winter sports. This is because a good combination of landscape and weather is rare.

Skiing weather

Skiing depends on good snow. Most people have to book their skiing holidays well in advance. So they want to know that there is a good chance that there will be plenty of snow and good sunny weather when they get to their destination.

The higher you are, the longer you can guarantee temperatures below freezing, the longer the snow lasts, and the longer the skiing season can be. This is why high mountains are the most favoured places for ski resorts (picture ①).

Skiing does not just depend on having snow, but on having the right kind of snow coupled with lots of sunshine. Very cold powdery snow makes for better skiing than

▼ ① These authorised skiing slopes are called pistes. Notice how they begin right outside the hotels of this high altitude ski resort.

wet snow. Heavy snowfalls can make skiing slopes almost unusable. And skiing is so much nicer in the sunshine than under cloud. As a result, the most attractive places have short snowstorms separated by long sunny periods – high, dry mountains.

Skiing locations

The higher up a mountain you go, the more difficult it is to get there and the more expensive everything will be. It will cost more to build hotels, it will cost more to bring in food and it will cost more to keep the roads clear of snow. This is why high altitude ski resorts are more expensive to stay in than those at lower altitudes (picture ②).

▼ ② **There isn't room for all ski resorts to be next to the pistes. Some have to be lower down the valleys.**

Safe pistes away from avalanche hazards.

The best resorts have good snowfall in occasional storms with long sunny intervals.

High-level resort close to pistes (more expensive to build and so dearer to stay in).

Ski lift

Low level resort. Cheaper accommodation but needs bus service to reach pistes.

◄ ③ **Even experts use safety equipment when they go mountaineering.**

The world's best winter sports

The combination of the reliable snow and good sunshine are hard to find.

Some places are simply too inaccessible (picture ③). As a result, the Himalayas, for example, are not winter sports centres.

Most winter sports centres are either near to where holidaymakers live or they are easy to get to. The best skiing in North America, for example, is thought to be in the Rocky Mountains, which have long sunny spells and fine, powdery snow. The best skiing in the Alps is often considered to be on the southern side, which has the most sunshine and the least wet snow.

Camping in the mountains

Mountains attract many people who want to have an outdoors holiday. But there are risks as well as benefits.

Millions of people visit mountains for their summer holidays each year and a large number of these go camping. Camping in the mountains is exciting because of the clear air and the scenery, but camping in some places does carry risks (picture ①).

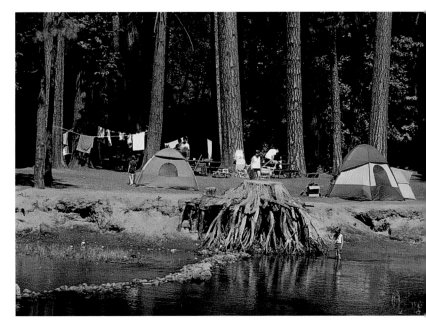

▲ ② **This is a safe, worry-free mountain campsite by a lake. Lake levels do not rise dramatically when it rains so flooding is unlikely. Camp fires, lit to help keep warm in the chilly evenings, can easily be made from 'dead and down' wood found near the trees.**

▼ ① **Some of the places where you can stay while camping in the mountains.**

Camping above the floodplain is safe.

Camping below cliffs can be risky because of the chance of rockfalls.

Camping here can be risky because the level in the river can rise quickly after a storm, flooding the campsite.

Camping near a lake is always safe because the water level changes only slowly.

This walker is wearing light clothing that will not be sufficient to guard against a rapid change in weather.

Camping by a stream below a lake is safe.

Risks of the valley floor

The flat land beside a river makes an attractive camping site (picture ②). But in some areas mountain weather can change quickly and a sunny day can be followed by days of rain or very heavy summer thunderstorms. The rain runs over the surface and gets into the mountain rivers very quickly, causing rivers to burst their banks and flood over their floodplains. This is a flash flood. The Pyrenees, the Alps, the Andes and the Rocky Mountains all have experienced many flash floods and fatalities in recent years.

In these circumstances, campers are particularly at risk. Valleys are narrow and water quickly floods across the bottom. Slopes may be too steep to climb and so people find themselves trapped (pictures ③ and ④).

On the mountains

Hiking up mountains from a valley campsite gives a glorious view and there are few people, so what might be the problems?

Mountain weather is notoriously changeable. A fine day can become stormy.

Many people also do not realise how quickly the temperature drops when the weather changes. Winds and rain-drenched clothing make it feel even colder, an effect called windchill. Severe windchill produces a life-threatening problem called hypothermia. So, it is always wise to pack good, warm, waterproof clothing – even in summer (picture ⑤).

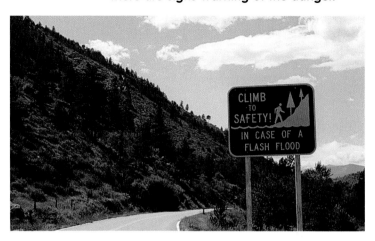

▼ ③ In flood-prone mountain valleys, there are signs warning of the danger.

▼ ④ Just because a river looks gentle in fine weather it does not mean it is always so. These pictures were both taken in August!

▼ ⑤ Hikers carrying packs with sufficient gear to enable them to camp in an emergency. Notice that they are wearing sensible clothing including long trousers to protect them from sunburn.

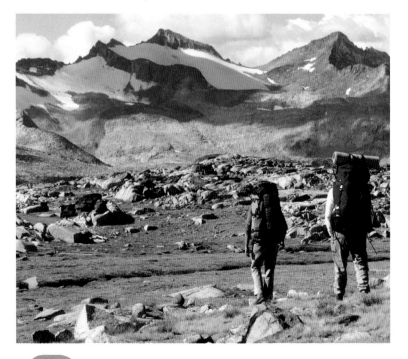

Mountain plants

Many mountain plants have to survive an extraordinarily harsh environment.

Mountain plants have to cope with cold, high winds, strong sunshine, driving rain, deep snow, ice, and thin, poor soils. To survive all this, mountain plants have to be tough. The higher up the mountains plants grow, the tougher they need to be (picture ①)

The forest zone

The lowest slopes of a mountain may be warm enough for trees like oak and ash to grow. They spread out their broad leaves in summer and shed them in winter. But farther up the slopes of a mountain, they are not found and, instead, the slopes are covered with conifers.

Near the top of the forest zone, conditions are too harsh even for conifers to grow well, and trees become more stunted (picture ③).

The treeless zone

Meadow plants thrive above the forest but, higher than this, only small and woody alpine plants can survive. These alpines hug the ground, or shelter between boulders. They are perennials, with a life of many years. Few annual plants grow here – it takes many years of slow, determined growth for a plant just to get big enough to flower (picture ②).

▼ ① **This diagram shows the main vegetation zones on a high mountain.**

Alpines

Few, if any plants can grow on the bare rocky cliffs at mountain tops.

Meadows

Tree line. The upper limit where a forest can grow.

Conifer trees, such as pine, firs and spruce grow up to the tree line. They may also be mixed with some hardy broadleaved trees, such as birch and aspen.

Forest zone

Broadleaved trees such as oak grow at the lowest altitudes.

Conifers are well adapted for long, cold winters and deep snowfalls. They have fine, downward-sloping needle-shaped leaves that readily shed the snow. The needles stay on from year to year because the growing season is too short for leaves to regrow each spring. The needles are dark-coloured to soak up as much heat as possible.

▼ ② **The many adaptations shown by plants high in the treeless zone.**

Alpines need to store as much heat as possible. Many are tufted, have furry leaves, and grow in dense, low bushes. Many even make their own antifreeze. The leaves are dark green to soak up as much of the sun's heat as possible.

Sedges and mosses grow where water was trapped and create bogs.

Hardy grasses

Edelweiss

Lichens cling to rocks.

Heather

Insulating snow cover protects plants in winter.

Thin, poor soils

All alpine plants need to be adapted for dry conditions. This may seem strange, when they may be covered in snow for half the year. But the water in snow is locked up as ice and so plants cannot use it. Then, as soon as the snow melts, harsh winds dry out the ground. To cope with this, even plants that seem tiny when seen on the surface may have deep tap roots that seek for water far underground.

Alpines have to make good use of the short growing season. As soon as the snow melts, they shoot, flower and set seed – giving the spectacular blossoms for which mountains are so famous. The entire growing season may be only 3 months.

▼ ③ **The many adaptations shown by plants in the forest zone. The hiker shows how big the plants are.**

Firs

Just above the tree line, summer meadows contain grasses and flowers. These bloom after the spring snowmelt.

Bilberry and mosses grow on the poor dark soils under the conifers.

Conifers have shallow roots that spread out to capture as much nourishment as possible from the thin soils. Conifers can also survive long winters when the ground is frozen hard and no water can reach the roots.

Weblink: www.CurriculumVisions.com

Mountain animals

Mountain animals are often seasonal visitors who move away during the harshest parts of winter. Those that stay for winter must be very hardy.

Plants have to stay wherever their seeds settle. But most animals can move around easily. As a result, far fewer animals live all year in mountains (pictures ①, ② and ③).

Migration

Animals like deer, bears, wolves, and large cats (such as mountain lions) spend the winter in the forests on the lowest slopes of the mountains, only venturing to higher altitudes in summer (picture ④).

Most animals that remain in the high mountains, such as marmots, settle down in the late autumn to hibernate until the snows melt in spring.

Large territories

Mountains are not a rich source of food for animals, because the plants are small and grow slowly. As a result, each animal has to have quite a large territory to find food. This is why mountains support only small numbers of animals. A single golden eagle, for example, needs a territory of 200 square kilometres just to find enough food for itself!

◀ ① With a wingspan of over 3 metres, the condor (which is a kind of vulture) is one of the world's largest flying birds. It uses its huge wing span to cruise high in the thin mountain air, and its excellent eyesight to find dead animals to eat.

▶ ② Mountain goats are extraordinarily agile climbers and are able to cross near-vertical rocky slopes to reach high pastures and to escape predators, such as mountain lions.

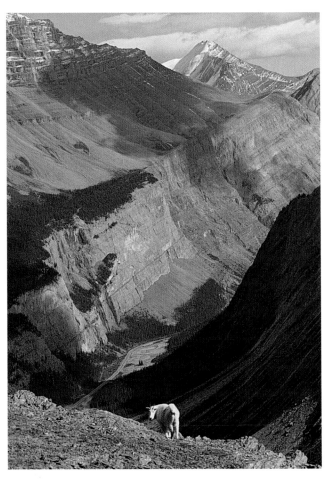

▼ ③ **This diagram shows some of the many adaptations of animals that help them to survive in the mountains.**

Golden eagle

Great height allows birds of prey to survey a large area – important when prey is scarce.

Mountain goats are skilled climbers and can navigate near-vertical cliffs to reach isolated patches of vegetation. However, even they must migrate to lower altitudes in winter because the high mountain areas are deeply covered in snow.

Cliff caves provide safe nesting sites and 'launch pads' for mountain birds such as eagles, condors and ravens.

Red deer venture out of the forests in summer.

In winter, ptarmigan do not hibernate. They scratch down through the snow to browse on shrubs and lichens. They burrow under the snow to protect themselves from the weather whilst they sleep.

Lynx

Raven

Ptarmigan

Few butterfly species are adapted to high altitudes because they need warmer conditions.

Marmot

Dipper is adapted to fast flowing mountain streams

It is common for animals that use camouflage to change their colour with the seasons. Ptarmigan and mountain hare both turn white in winter. In summer, they are patterned brown.

Mountain hare

Apollo butterfly

Many rodents in high mountains live in a network of tunnels in the bouldery soil. These provide a place to hibernate in winter. However, as the rodents search among the rocks for food, they are easily spotted by predators such as eagles, weasels, lynx and foxes. To escape being caught, they scurry into the shelter of rocks.

▲ ④ **Bears eat both plants and animals. They are able to move to lower altitudes in the winter. Even then, they may hibernate in a den for the coldest part of the year.**

Weblink: www.CurriculumVisions.com

Protecting mountain environments

Mountains are attractive places for a holiday, but as more and more people visit them, they are under increasing threat.

Many people do not realise how fragile the mountain environment is. They imagine that, because there are rocks about, the land is indestructible. But, an important part of the environment is the soil and wildlife, and these are much more fragile.

Fragile soils and plants

Mountain soils are thin, often full of water, and move when trodden on (picture ①). Because mountain plants grow very slowly, they cannot stand up to even moderate trampling.

If many people walk over mountain meadows and alpine plants, the plants will soon be damaged and die back, leaving the soil exposed. The soft soil is then easily washed away. Even skiing on snow can damage the plants below so that, when the spring comes, they cannot grow again (picture ②).

Problems for animals

Many animals are extremely shy and cannot tolerate large numbers of people. Wherever there are people, these animals will be driven away and forced into more and more remote places, where their food may be scarce. This will upset the delicate balance of nature.

On the other hand, some wild animals get used to eating the scraps left by human visitors when they picnic or camp (picture ③).

▼ ① **Examples of the damage that people can do to the mountain environment.**

People being careless with cigarettes and matches can cause fires.

Trampling damages plant growth and leaves the soil bare. The bare soils are then easily eroded.

Acid rain from nearby cities damages or kills sensitive plants such as lichens.

Pollutants in the air can get held in snow. When the ice melts, the pollutants seep down into the soil with the water and are taken up by the roots of plants.

Litter, such as cans and plastic wrappers, does not rot in the environment and can be a hazard to animals.

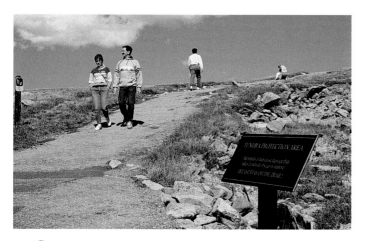

▲ ② **Providing marked and well-maintained paths reduces the impact of visitors on popular places.**

If any animal comes to depend on scraps in the summer it will be less able to look after itself in the winter when there are no people about. Some may even die.

Preserving the wilderness

If we want the natural world to survive, we have to leave some mountain areas unvisited. We must learn that we cannot always put our own interests ahead of other living things on this earth. This is why governments create wilderness areas, and why our surviving wilderness must be protected (picture ④).

◄ ③ **It may seem kind to feed animals such as deer. But this attracts them to people and makes them more likely to be involved in traffic accidents. If wild animals eat too much human food, they can become ill. They may also be less able to fend for themselves during the winter when there are no tourists about.**

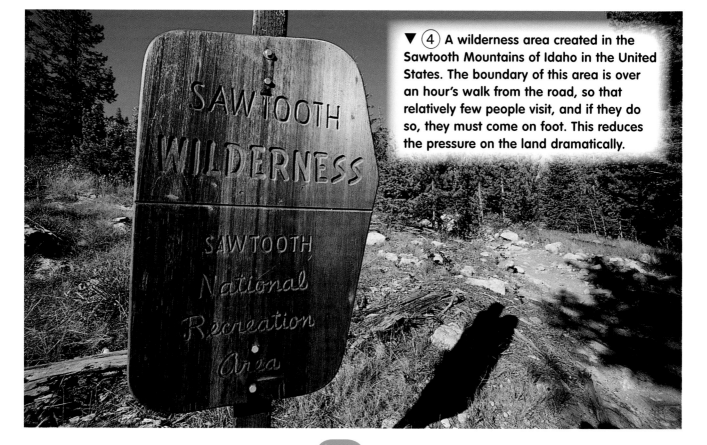

▼ ④ **A wilderness area created in the Sawtooth Mountains of Idaho in the United States. The boundary of this area is over an hour's walk from the road, so that relatively few people visit, and if they do so, they must come on foot. This reduces the pressure on the land dramatically.**

Weblink: www.CurriculumVisions.com

Living on the roof of the world

The weather in the world's high mountains is full of contrasts.

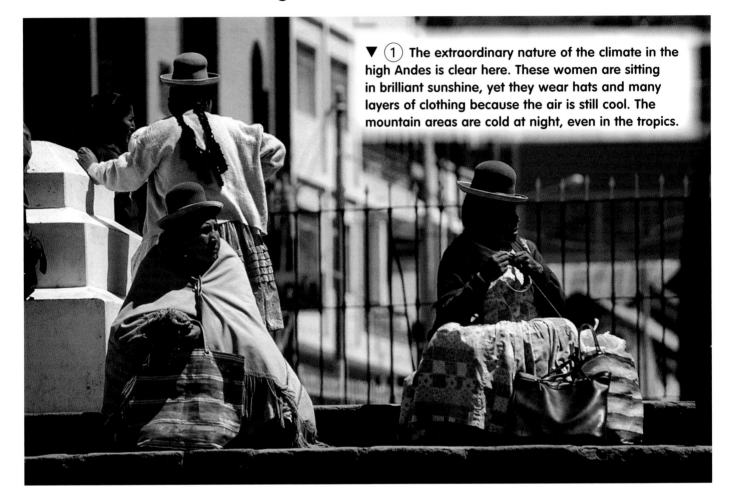

▼ (1) The extraordinary nature of the climate in the high Andes is clear here. These women are sitting in brilliant sunshine, yet they wear hats and many layers of clothing because the air is still cool. The mountain areas are cold at night, even in the tropics.

Imagine that you have gone for a holiday to Lake Titicaca in the equatorial Andes mountains of Peru. Before you go, you look up the weather on the Internet, but the nearest station you can find is at sea level. Here, it is forecast to be hot and steamy. You know that temperatures fall with altitude, so you suppose your mountain destination will be pleasantly mild. But you are in for a shock!

Thin air

You get out at the airport 4,000 metres up in the mountains. You immediately find it difficult to breathe. This is not what you had expected. You have a headache and cannot work out why.

Someone tells you it is altitude sickness because your brain is not getting enough oxygen. This is because the air is far thinner than at sea level and so each breath contains less oxygen. It will take days for your body to adjust and for the headache to go away.

Bright sunshine

The sun shines from an intensely blue sky and the glare hurts your eyes. The air is so clear, you can see for huge distances. This is because there is much less dust to block out the sun.

It feels warm in the sunshine. You move into the shade to get out of the glare and

◀ ③ In the high Andes, each day is a mixture of morning sunshine and afternoon thundershowers. There can be truly 'four seasons in one day'.

▶ ② While holidaymakers on the coast at the equator bask in warm sunshine, these ferrymen are dressed for the cold on Lake Titicaca in Peru. At over 3,800 m above sea level, temperatures can fall well below freezing at night. During the day, however, the skies are clear and, despite the chill in the air, a strong sun makes it feel pleasant.

feel cold, even though it is summer. This is because the thinner air cannot soak up the heat as much as the air near to sea level and so it remains cold (pictures ① and ②).

Changeable weather

The wind begins to howl. Your face feels dry and your lips begin to crack. This is because the air has far less moisture in it than at sea level.

Suddenly, without warning, thunderclouds appear (picture ③). Hailstones bounce off the ground. Then, just as quickly, the clouds pass and it is sunny again.

Cold night

The sun begins to set. As soon as darkness comes, the temperature of the air plummets and all the streams freeze over. You begin to shiver and need to be indoors. You have to remind yourself you are still at the equator.

You look around and begin to understand better why the people have weather-beaten skin like leather, and why they have warm clothes and wide-brimmed hats. You soon realise that the local people know just how best to live in this extraordinary weather.

Mountain farming

**Mountains have a harsh climate, steep slopes and poor soil.
All these call for special dedication from the farmers.**

Mountains do not provide the best farmland. The climate is cool or cold, rainfall is high and it is often cloudy. The growing season is short, and the soils are thin and often infertile. It is rarely possible to grow crops. This is why mountain farmers are mostly pastoralists who rear livestock (picture ①).

Summer on the farm

During the summer, animals can graze the mountain pastures (picture ②). This also allows the best valley land to be used for growing the grass, which will be cut and stored for winter feed (picture ③).

▼ ① **The shape of the land affects what a farmer does. When the summer grazing is close to the farm (as on the bottom right of the diagram), it is sufficient to simply turn the animals loose on the mountains. But, when the grazing is far away, people and animals have to live away from the farm during the summer.**

In places such as the Himalayas where mountain pastures are a long way from the farm, some of the farm family and animals spend summer on distant high-level pastures.

The seasonal movement of people and animals is called transhumance.

Farms in valley close to most fertile land and in most sheltered position

In places such as the Lake District where mountain pastures are close to the farm, animals spend summer grazing on nearby low mountains.

▼ ② A mountain farm in the Himalayas. This is the summer mountain pasture. Children and grandparents spend the summer on these high pastures with their sheep and goats. It takes many days to get down to the valley farm, so the journey is made only at the start and end of the summer. This is transhumance.

▼ ④ A mountain farm in the Lake District. Here you can see the farm buildings huddled together to provide winter shelter. The best pastures and fields for hay are close to the farm. All around are the poorer grazing lands of the mountains.

Winter on the farm

Winter conditions are harsh (picture ④). Animals may freeze if left out on the mountains, so they have to be brought back to the shelter of the farm buildings.

During the winter, animals have to be fed from supplies that the farmer has gathered during the summer.

Making ends meet

Mountain farming is not a way to get rich. Many farmers find it very difficult to make enough money. To make up their incomes, they often have to do some other work. They may have a wintertime job in the valleys, or they may have to use their farms in other ways, such as opening them as guesthouses to summer tourists.

◄ ③ Mountain farmers in the Alps also take their animals to summer mountain pastures, although very few live in high alpine huts, but drive up to the fields from the towns each day.

▲ ⑤ Early winter snowfall is a sign that animals will have to be brought into the shelter of the farmyard.

Homes for a mountain winter

People build special kinds of homes to survive the harshness of the winter.

Mountains have some of the world's most severe weather. In general, the higher up a mountain people live, the colder and windier it gets, and the longer they have to cope with snow. In these circumstances keeping warm is a high priority and everyone who lives in the mountains has a high fuel bill.

In very high mountains, snow may lie for many months and an ordinary house will not be warm enough. Mountain houses have to be built for mountain weather (picture ①).

▼ ① **These are the deep snow conditions that people in the mountains have to cope with. It is important to build roofs that make good use of the winter snow. Steeply sloping roofs would shed the snow and make the roofs cold. A gently sloping roof keeps a layer of snow, which acts as a natural blanket.**

Traditional homes

People in the past had to be self-sufficient. They had to care for their animals as well as for themselves throughout the long, harsh winters. They might find themselves cut off for months on end. So they had to make sure they had enough food and fuel for themselves and their animals (pictures ②, ③ and ④).

Modern homes

Modern homes in the mountains have thick insulation, but with modern materials, walls do not have to be as thick as in the past, so they look like ordinary homes. Triple glazing allows windows to be large and let in lots of light during the winter and yet still keep out the cold.

◀ ② This traditional stone house is in the Italian Alps. Notice the tiny windows in the bottom floor (where the animals were kept) and the avalanche protection fences behind. The front door is reached by a tall staircase so that it is free of snow all winter. The walls are made of thick stone to help keep in the heat.

▶ ③ An alternative to thick stone walls is to build in wood. Wood is a good insulator, and wooden houses are easier to build than stone houses.

Wood is also winter fuel. It is stacked within the house so that it can be reached easily even when the houses are snowed in.

▼ ④ In some places, the bottom floor of many mountain farmhouses was used entirely for animals. Throughout the winter, animals and people lived together, keeping one another warm.

Ramp entrance

Storage for wood, food and other essentials

Hay loft

Roof juts out to shelter the building from snow.

Living space

Pigs

Cellar

Cows

Slope

Where towns are found

The local climate and landscape vary enormously in mountain areas. People have learnt how to live where conditions are best.

In cold environments it is vital to make the very best use of the environment to stay warm and safe.

Making the most of the weather

The most critical part of each day is early morning. The valley is very cold because, overnight, bitterly cold air rolls down from the surrounding snowy mountains (picture ①).

Each day the sun rises in the southeast and shines first on the northwestern (southeast-facing) slopes. So this is the side where the frost and snow melt fastest and where the pastures have the best grass.

Many people try to live on the slopes facing the morning sun (picture ③). Others try to live on slopes away from valley bottoms so that they don't spend the night surrounded by cold air.

Choosing a safe site

Landslides and avalanches are common in mountain valleys, but, by looking carefully at the shape of the land, people can see where the safest places are. For example, people can avoid places where the shape of the land makes a natural funnel for moving soil or snow.

▼ ① **The site of towns in mountain regions.**

Slopes facing northwest stay in shadow for the longest time.

Valley bottom gets an overnight pool of cold air that has rolled down from the mountain top.

No towns are built near places where landslides and avalanches are common.

Town on valley side facing southeast gets early morning warmth of the sun.

Town sited off valley floor to protect it from spring and summer floods.

SE

NW

Many towns are built below forests because trees take the impact of a landslide or avalanche.

In spring, when the snows often melt suddenly, there is also the threat of flooding. Many towns are built above the river floodplain for this reason (picture ②).

▶ ② **This village is sited on a natural bench that is clear of the cold valley bottom and away from river flooding.**

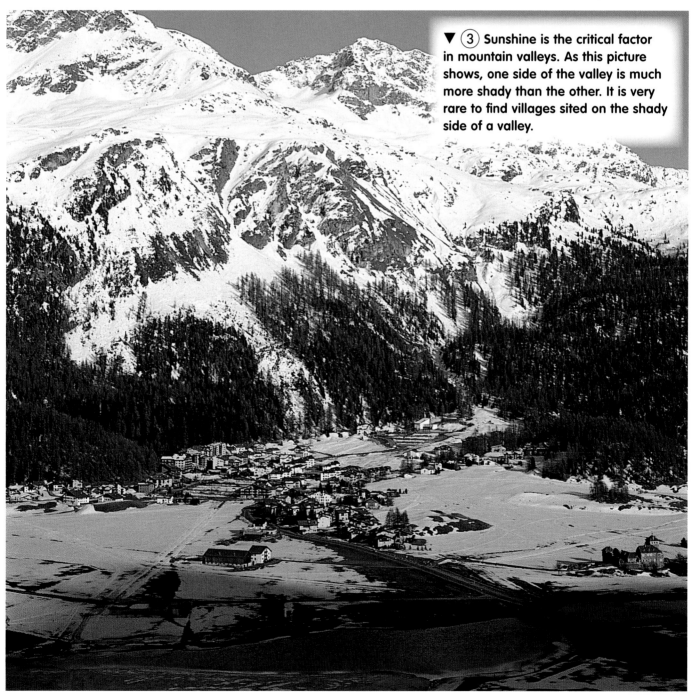

▼ ③ **Sunshine is the critical factor in mountain valleys. As this picture shows, one side of the valley is much more shady than the other. It is very rare to find villages sited on the shady side of a valley.**

41

Routes through the mountains

With steep slopes, high peaks and harsh weather, it is very difficult to get about in mountains. Here we see what it is like in the Alps..

Travel in mountains can be difficult because of steep slopes and bad winter weather. As a result, people have had to build special roads and railways to cross mountains (pictures ① and ②).

Travel and landscape

Connecting valleys is especially difficult. Most routes use passes (see page 19).

To reach the passes, roads often have to be built with many hairpin bends, just to make a slope gentle enough for vehicles to use.

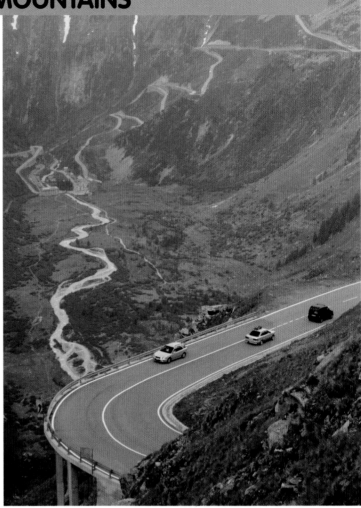

▲ ① **Crossing this alpine valley has required the building of switchback roads with many hairpin bends.**

Avalanche tunnel to protect road

Route over pass reached by hairpin bends. Closed in winter

Avalanche hazard

Main roads and railways in tunnels and on bridges. These are very expensive to build.

Chance of storms, blizzards and snowdrifts

Risk of snow closing road in winter

◀▲ ② **Some of the ways in which people have created routes through mountains and the hazards they face.**

▼E ③ Sometimes the only way to get about is to blast a tunnel through the mountainside. Notice that the entrance to the tunnel in the picture below has a special roof to protect the road from avalanches.

Train travel is sometimes possible, but only with trains designed for the steep gradients.

If the route is important, tunnels are blasted through the mountains, and roads are carried across valleys and gorges on bridges (picture ③). But this is very expensive.

▼ ④ In the alps, high mountain passes may be closed from November to May by the deep snow.

Travel and weather

The weather can be just as much of a problem as the landscape. In winter, snow drifts in valleys and across passes. Snow can fall far faster than it can be cleared away by even the most powerful modern machines, and most of the high mountain passes are shut throughout the winter months (picture ④). Avalanches are a real hazard in late winter and spring, when the snow is very thick and slides easily down slopes.

Seeking a fortune from the mountains

One of the times when mountains attract many people is when gold and silver are found. At such times, both people and the mountain environment may suffer terribly.

When mountains are being formed, great heat and pressure cause some of the rocks to melt. In this way, precious metals like gold and silver become concentrated into bands called mineral veins.

In time, the mountains are worn down and the metals are exposed at the surface and washed into the river where they settle on the river bed.

The rush for wealth

In the past, the discovery of mountain gold and silver has caused hundreds of thousands of people to rush to seek their fortunes. The most famous of them was the gold rush that occurred in the Klondike River valley in the Rocky Mountains of Canada (pictures ① and ②).

▼ ① **Mining life for the goldrush miners in areas such as the Klondike River in the Rockies.**

Steep slopes made it hard for miners to bring their gear in and their gold out.

Many miners died from cold because they had poor protection from the winter weather.

Severe winter weather meant they could not mine the frozen ground in winter.

Timber was used by miners, so they cut down large areas of forest.

Waste from the smelting processes was left to pollute the land.

Mining was a matter of sorting the gold from the gravel in and around the river. This is called panning.

▲ ② **Most of the gold was won from the beds of rivers that flowed in the mountains. This miner is washing the river gravel to separate gold from rock.**

Mountain weather and miners

Most miners had left their city jobs in the hope of making their fortunes. They did not understand how severe mountain weather could be, nor how difficult it was to travel in the mountains. In the Klondike it was over 1000 kilometres on foot from the nearest port to where the gold was found.

They were faced with the hazards of deep snow, blizzards, freezing cold and avalanches. The miners had only tents to live in, and many died of the cold.

Those who struck lucky had enormous wealth which they spent on building towns in the high mountains. Everything had to be imported at vast expense for these 'boom towns'.

▶ ③ **Snow cloaks an abandoned mine in the Rocky Mountains. It gives a good idea of how harsh winter conditions could be for miners.**

Mountain pollution

The metals the miners dug from the ground were often mixed up with waste rock.

For this reason miners extracted metal from rock as close to the mines as possible. They cut down forests for fuel and left piles of waste to pollute the ground. Over a century later, still nothing will grow on these waste tips.

Ghost towns

In the end, the gold and silver were worked out. So, people drifted away to seek their fortunes somewhere else, and the mining towns went bust. Many were abandoned and are often no more than ghost towns today (picture ③).

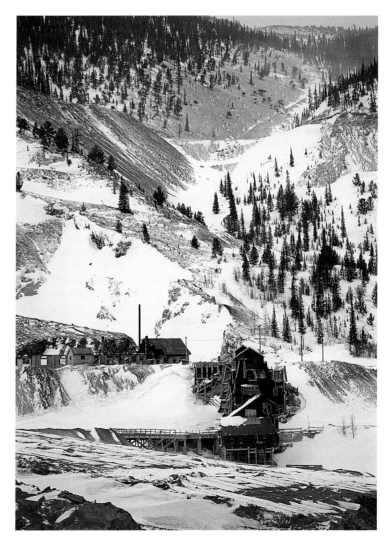

Glossary

ALPINES A word used to refer to plants that grow in cold, high mountain environments where there is a long period of seasonal snow cover, and where the plants have to stand up to wind, cold and drought as well as to thin, infertile soils. These plants are usually small and ground hugging.

ALTITUDE The height above sea level, measured in metres (or feet).

ALTITUDE SICKNESS Also known as mountain sickness. It is an illness people get when they go up to a high altitude too quickly. It is caused by a lack of oxygen to the brain and muscles. This makes people feel dizzy, short of breath and very tired.

ANNUAL PLANT A plant that only lives for a year or less.

ARETE A word for a mountain ridge. *See* **RIDGE**.

AVALANCHE A rapid movement of snow down a steep mountainside. Avalanches are extremely powerful, contain millions of tonnes of material and move at over 300 km/hr. They mainly occur in spring when snow thicknesses are highest.

BLIZZARD A weather condition of driving snow in winds exceeding 50 km/hr. Drifting snow is a common feature of a blizzard.

BROADLEAF TREE A tree that has relatively wide and flat leaves. Contrasts with conifers that have needle-shaped leaves. Most broadleaf trees in places with a cold winter shed their leaves in the autumn (deciduous).

CIRQUE Another name for a corrie. *See* **CORRIE**.

CONIFER A tree that bears cones and needle-shaped leaves. Conifers include firs, spruce and pines and all are found on mountains. Conifers have many adaptations to withstand cold, dry winters, heavy snowfalls, and a short growing season. Most do not shed their leaves at one time of the year (they are evergreen).

CORNICE A wedge of snow that builds up on the sheltered side of a mountain peak.

CORRIE A glacially scoured bowl or saucer-shaped hollow in a high mountainside. Other names include cirque (French) and cwm (Welsh).

CRUST The earth's crust is the outer brittle rocks of the earth. The crust makes up the top part of the giant plates that move slowly across the surface of the earth.

EROSION The wearing away and removal of land.

FINGER LAKE A long lake that takes on the shape of a glaciated valley. Most finger lakes fill hollows on valleys scoured out by ancient glaciers. Some have been created where they have flooded the valley upstream of a moraine.

FLASH FLOOD A flood which occurs suddenly and without warning. Flash floods are common after torrential mountain thunderstorms. They affect mountain valleys because there is little soil to soak up the rain and so the water quickly rushes to rivers.

FLOOD When a river bursts its banks.

FLOODPLAIN The flat land on either side of a river, made up of materials deposited by the river in times of flood.

FOLD An arched-up layer of rock. Rocks that are arched up are called anticlines and those that are arched down are called synclines.

FOLD MOUNTAIN A mountain whose rocks are mainly formed from folding of rock layers. This separates them from volcanic mountains whose rocks are formed from ash and lava.

FROST SHATTER The way in which bare rock is broken away from a mountainside by the seasonal freezing and thawing of water.

GLACIER A large tongue of ice that flows down a slope. A glacier which flows entirely within a valley is sometimes called a valley glacier. If a glacier comes out of mountains and spreads out onto a plain, it becomes part of an ice sheet. If valley glaciers fill their valleys during an ice age, the ice spills over the crests to make a mountain ice cap, or, if larger, a mountain ice sheet.

GOLD RUSH The rapid migration, or rush, of people to a newly discovered goldfield. People who joined a gold rush hoped to become very rich. A few did but most didn't.

HAIRPIN BEND A sharp U-shaped bend in the road where it turns back on itself. Hairpin bends are most common where roads go up or down very steep slopes. The part of a road with a hairpin bend is called a switchback.

HANGING VALLEY A valley that ends abruptly, overlooking a deep U-shaped valley. Many hanging valleys have waterfalls issuing from them.

HAZARD An event that might cause a threat to people or property. Avalanches, floods, rockfalls and being caught out in cold weather are among the most common mountain hazards.

HIBERNATE Some animals go into a state where they go to sleep for a long period and their bodies slow right down. This allows them to survive the winter when there would be little food about.

HORN A sharp-pointed peak. It is sometimes called a pyramidal peak because it is shaped like a pyramid. *See also* **PEAK**.

HYPOTHERMIA A cooling of the inner part of a person's body such that their life is threatened.

ICE AGE A period of time, beginning about 2 million years ago, when it was common, from time to time, for glaciers to surge down from mountains and form ice sheets. At present, glaciers and ice sheets have shrunk back, but it is likely they will grow again.

INFERTILE SOIL A soil that contains so little nourishment that few plants will grow on it, and even those that do grow contain little nourishment for animals that might feed on them. Infertile soils will not produce crops.

INSULATION Materials used to reduce the loss of heat from a house. For example, fibrous materials that trap air can be put into wall cavities, and the seal around doors and windows carefully filled.

LANDSCAPE Another word for a particular type of scenery. For example, a mountain landscape has high peaks, sharp ridges and steeply sloping valleys.

LANDSLIDE A rapid sliding of rock and soil on a steep mountain slope.

LEE SIDE The side of a mountain or a range of mountains that is sheltered from the prevailing winds.

MINERAL VEIN A band of rock containing a large proportion of valuable metal. Another word used for a mineral vein is *lode*.

MOISTURE The amount of water held in the air as invisible vapour. In this state, water is a gas.

MORAINE A ridge of rubbly stones, boulders and fine clay left behind when a glacier or ice sheet melts.

MOUNTAIN An area of land that stands up from the surrounding countryside by at least 300 m.

MOUNTAIN CHAIN The term for many ranges of fold mountains of similar age that were formed at the same time as each other and form a wide belt running across a continent. Also called a mountain system or mountain belt.

MOUNTAIN ENVIRONMENT The landscape, climate and wildlife that are found in mountains.

MOUNTAIN RANGE A short line of mountain peaks linked together by continuous high land.

PASS A lower gap through the crest of a mountain range made by the scouring action of a glacier or the downcutting by a large river. To be a pass, the gap has to provide a useful link for people to travel from one side of the mountains to the other.

PASTORALIST A farmer whose livelihood comes from rearing animals.

PEAK A sharp-pointed mountain summit. Rounded summits are not peaks.

PERENNIAL PLANT A plant that lives for several years and not just one year.

PLATE Also known as tectonic plate, this is the name for a piece of the earth's crust that is separated from other pieces of crust by fractures in the earth's surface.

POLLUTION The contamination of the air, the snow or the water by artificial substances such as gases and liquids. Much mountain pollution comes in from the air in the form of gases that can cause acid rain or acid snow.

RAINSHADOW EFFECT The way in which a mountain range blocks the path of air and forces the air to rise and release its moisture on the windward side, leaving very little moisture left for the leeward side. The leeward side is the rainshadow side of the mountain.

RESORT A place where people visit for recreation. The type of recreation is normally added to the word resort, for example, ski resort, mountain resort, beach resort, etc.

RIBBON LAKE Another word for finger lake. *See* **FINGER LAKE**.

RIDGE A long, often sharp-edged crest in a mountain range (also known as an arete).

SCREE Broken fragments of rock that have been shattered from mountains by winter frosts.

SEASON A part of the year which has its own characteristic weather. In the tropics, where it is always warm, there are wet seasons and dry seasons. Elsewhere, the seasons (summer, autumn, winter and spring) are based on temperature.

SNOWDRIFT A place where the wind has piled up the snow so that it is exceptionally thick. Snowdrifts are common in front of, and behind, obstructions such as houses and fences.

SNOWLINE The line at which snow lies. The snowline changes through the year, becoming higher in the summer, when conditions are warm, and then sinking lower with the onset of winter.

TAP ROOT A central root of a plant that goes straight down into the ground in search of water.

TERRITORY A part of the landscape an animal regards as its home space. An animal marks out and defends its territory by, for example, calls, or by fighting with intruders.

TRANSHUMANCE A type of traditional mountain farming where animals are taken to high pastures for the summer season when the snow has melted and then brought back down again as soon as the weather starts to worsen.

TRIBUTARY A small part, or branch, of a river or glacier.

U-SHAPED VALLEY A valley which has been scoured by a glacier. The 'U' refers to the shape you see when you look up or down a glacially-scoured valley.

VEGETATION ZONE A distinctive group of plants that live between certain heights up the side of a mountain.

VOLCANO A mountain made of layers of ash and lava. The classic volcano is shaped like a cone.

V-SHAPED VALLEY A river valley with straight sides and one that looks like the letter V.

WEATHER The short-term nature of the atmosphere. We describe the weather in terms of the sunshine, rain, wind, cloud, temperature, fog, etc.

WILDERNESS An area which is still mainly untouched by people.

WINDCHILL An effect caused by strong wind. The wind can carry away heat from unprotected skin, and this, in turn, can make the body very cold. Severe windchill can lead to people suffering from hypothermia.

WINDWARD SIDE The side of a mountain or a range of mountains that faces the prevailing winds.

Index